AFREE-MEEH

"Freedom from History Enslavement."

By Shamara Smith

EBOOK: 978-1-966131-52-6

PAPERBACK: 978-1-966131-53-3

Published by **Author Publications**: 2025

https://www.authorpublications.com

+1 (771) 203-5560

Printed in the United States of America

Table of Contents

About Meeh

My name is Shamara Smith, a young woman on a journey of self-discovery. In 2020, after exploring different genres of music and experiencing a period of reflection and spiritual exploration, I felt compelled to understand my roots on a deeper level. This led me to take a DNA test, and I was astounded that my ancestry roots to Africa. From that moment, my mission became clear: to honor my heritage and, through AFREE~MEEH, to build a movement that challenges the distorted system affecting us, the people of color.

AFREE~MEEH is first an expression to be freed for anyone who feels cramped up in the years-old system built around them—a call to rise up, assert our freedom, and strive for a free world that reflects the strength and unity of Africa. With this mini-book, I intend to provide a guide for those who want to break free from the shackles of historical and societal oppression. With the turn of each page, you would discover some deep-rooted systemic norms that deprived the people of color of their rights for eons, leading you to disclosure. May these words inspire you to embrace your strength and be a beacon for those seeking "Freedom From History Enslavement."

Meeh and the Bible

Beliefs are innate though acquirable, a deeply personal idea woven into our system from the seeds of our upbringing, our past experiences and our pursuit of meaning. They should be ours to explore and understand without any pressure. It should not be imposed by others around. Growing up, I was raised to believe in a divine force that is God and Jesus, and the church played a central role in my family's life. I remember people from the church community would visit our yard and would urge us to join Bible study, speaking of how they turned their lives around with salvation and guidance found within the scriptures. Eventually, my family gave in. I remember the feeling of sitting down in that first Bible study session, learning about the books from Deuteronomy to Mark, and discovering the rich stories within each chapter. It was an introduction to faith through the pages of the Bible, where lessons, parables, and history mingled, creating a moral framework that would guide us in the years ahead.

My grandmother from my dad's side, especially, nurtured our spiritual journey. She was the heart of our Sunday mornings, waking us with the joy of church service and making sure we were mindfully present and involved.

Every other Sunday, I'd watch her stand at the church doors, welcoming guests and congregation members alike. Her role as an usher seemed like more than a responsibility; it was a symbol of service and dedication, a quiet expression of her belief in love and community. Later, at the age of fourteen, I made the decision to be baptized, a milestone that felt like both a promise and a transformation. It was surreal!

I remember the jitters before getting baptized, standing before the congregation, then feeling the water around immersing me, cool and reassuring, as I was dipped in what I believed to be holy waters. That moment was a declaration: I was cleansed, renewed, free from sin. But the world around me was still filled with temptation, and despite this new beginning, I soon realized the struggle with sin was far from over. As the years passed, I began to understand that my baptism did not shield me from the evil realities of the world. The journey was just beginning, with new questions arising at every turn.

The Journey from Innocence to Awareness

As children, we rarely have the capacity—or perhaps the reason—to ponder the weight of life's complexities. Days flow by in a rhythm of exploration, each one filled with toys, laughter, and the irresistible pull of whatever gadget or game catches our attention. Life feels boundless and safe, a bright mosaic of moments that seem endless. We are far too busy living in those moments to ever consider the vastness of reality or the hidden truths waiting beyond the edges of childhood.

I used to believe that the world would always stay that simple and that I'd have plenty of time before I'd need to worry or understand more. But growing up changes things in ways we can't foresee. It brings moments that gently—or sometimes abruptly—pull back the curtain, forcing us to see that life isn't just what we imagine it to be as children. Reality is not as controllable or forgiving as we once thought.

I remember when it hit me, that first moment when I realized I'd have to navigate the world alone, that some things I'd go through would be mine alone to carry. And in that realization, I felt a strange mixture of fear and freedom. Fear because there's a stark loneliness in realizing that life's hardest truths are yours to face alone. Freedom, because with this realization comes the power to define my own journey, understanding that even if life is beyond my control, how I walk through it belongs solely to me.

It wasn't until I was nearing 32 that I discovered a detail about myself: I was born a premature baby. The revelation came almost as a shock as if a hidden piece of my identity had suddenly been unearthed. I found myself reflecting on why this detail, which felt so significant, had been concealed for so long. Was it something my family deemed too inconsequential to share, or did they think I might not fully understand its importance?

Perhaps they intended to protect me, thinking it would not change who I had become or the life I had lived. Yet I couldn't help but wonder how differently I might have viewed my life if I'd known sooner—at a time like 18, when adulthood begins to unfold, and we start to think seriously about our health, our journey, and our place in the world. Knowing this at such a formative age might have allowed me to see my life in a different light, perhaps with more gratitude for my resilience or a deeper commitment to cherishing each day. But here I was, years later, piecing together parts of myself that had always been there yet were somehow unfamiliar.

It made me think about the importance of truth and how understanding our own story—even the parts that are difficult or unexpected—can provide clarity and a profound sense of self-acceptance. Discovering that I was premature allowed me to reflect not only on my beginnings but on the incredible, sometimes invisible, resilience we carry with us, hidden beneath the surface until we are ready to see it.

Now, with both my parents gone, the sense of solitude in my journey has deepened. In their absence, I've been left to sift through fragments of memories and unanswered questions, wondering about the things they might have shared if they'd had the chance. The thought that knowing about my premature birth might have shaped my perspective on life sooner now feels both poignant and bittersweet.

I'm left contemplating all the things I would have done differently had I understood more about my beginnings and about the significance of having one's life stretched out before them like an unwritten map. Without them here to guide me, I have come to understand the weight and beauty of knowing oneself fully and the importance of passing that knowledge down to those who will come after. I realize now that in a world where time is fleeting, and certainty is rare, awareness can be a kind of anchor.

Knowledge of oneself, of one's roots and early experiences, isn't just a tool for navigating life; it's a way to honor the journey and face both life and death with clarity and strength. For those who follow, I want to emphasize how knowing your own story, from its earliest moments to its hardest truths, can save you heartache and guide you through life's inevitable storms. In the end, we face our lives alone, each of us in solitude, whether in life or in death. And while we may carry the love and wisdom of those who came before us, it is our own understanding of self that lights the path forward, even when all else fades away.

In the absence of my parents, I now feel a bigger responsibility to those who will walk this path after me. My experiences, my struggles, my realizations—they aren't just my own anymore. They're a part of a broader story, a lineage of knowledge and resilience that needs to be shared.

If I could impart one lesson to those who come after me, it would be the importance of understanding our own stories, even the parts we might initially wish to ignore or overlook.

Because knowledge, when rooted in truth, has a power unlike anything else—it can shape our choices, strengthen our resolve, and protect us from the unknown hazards that life so often presents. Learning about my own beginnings so late in life left me with a sense of what might have been, a lingering "what if" that I hope those who come after won't have to carry.

Life and death are the two certainties we all face, unyielding and ultimately beyond our control. In both of these realities, we are alone, facing the end or beginning of our journey with only what we've learned and what we carry within us. Yet, within that solitude, there is also a gift—a chance to define ourselves on our own terms, to embrace the things we've endured and make sense of them. I hope to instill in those who follow the understanding that life is precious and fleeting and that the only true security we have lies in knowing ourselves deeply.

To face life with awareness is to be prepared for its challenges; to face death with acceptance is to find peace, even in the unknown. In this cycle of life and death, each generation stands alone yet connected, drawing from the wisdom of the past while carving a path for the future.

Exploring Questions of Faith and Reality

Now, in my thirties, I find myself going deeper and deeper into questioning everything around me, which I never paid any heed to before. My faith has grown, but as I explored more, it becomes more complex. Today, I seek understanding rooted in both my spiritual beliefs and the realities I've experienced. I've ran into Wu-Sabat. A class based upon facts bringing me to a question: *If Jesus sacrificed himself to save us from sin, why does sin still exist in the world?* It's a question that challenges me as it contrasts the certainty of religious teachings with the uncertainty of everyday life.

If sin still prevails in this world despite his sacrifice, then what did it mean for him to die for humanity's sins? Sometimes, I wonder if it would have made more sense if we had all been born at one age and remained that way—unchanging, untouched by the progression of time. If that were the case, we might not experience different stages in life that challenge our morals or tempt us to stray from a righteous path. We wouldn't be faced with the struggles of youth, adulthood, or the weight of responsibility that often leads us to question or even contradict our beliefs. In that unchanging state, Jesus' sacrifice might feel more tangible, a salvation that remains constant rather than tested by the trials of life.

Another question that puzzles me is the idea of judgment. If Jesus died to save us, then why are we still subject to judgment? The Bible teaches that our actions on earth are measured and that each person will stand accountable for their life. Yet, if we are saved, why are we still evaluated by the standards of sin and righteousness? This has led me to wonder about the very purpose of salvation and its implications for our lives. Is salvation a promise that frees us or a responsibility we are meant to carry, living in a way that continually justifies that sacrifice?

Tracing Beliefs Beyond the Bible

When I think about the origins of these beliefs, I am reminded that the Bible did not originate with my ancestors. Its teachings came to Africa through the influence of missionaries and colonization, and with it came a set of stories that didn't entirely reflect the history or beliefs of my heritage. For example, in the Bible, Adam and Eve are described as the first humans created by God, yet they are unlike the people I know, the people of Africa, whose history stretches back far beyond what the Bible narrates.

9

This raises questions: *Who were my ancestors before they were taught the stories of Adam and Eve? What were their beliefs, their values, and their understanding of the divine?*

The narrative of Adam and Eve itself raises profound questions. According to the Bible, all of humanity descended from this single pair, but as I ponder, I'm led to question the logic of this story. We are taught that men come from women, not the other way around. In our lives, it is the woman who gives birth, bringing forth life. So, how could Eve, the first woman, have been created from Adam? Further into the story, we read about Cain and Abel, the sons of Adam and Eve, but who were their wives? If humanity began with only Adam and Eve, then who did their children marry? Were there other people on Earth beyond the biblical family? So many swirling questions often lead us to question the very beginning of everything: The rise of Adam and Eve.

How are we supposed to be God-like without a god? This is the result in which the so called Adam and Eve messed up.

These questions take me back to Africa, to a history that predates biblical records. What beliefs did African societies hold before the Bible was introduced? Many African cultures held complex spiritual beliefs and a deep respect for nature, recognizing a higher power or forces that governed life and community. These beliefs, passed down through generations, may not have been written in holy books, but they were no less sacred or meaningful. They connected people to their ancestors, to the land, and to the mysteries of existence in ways that perhaps cannot be captured within the pages of a single book.

The Bible Genesis: The Cause and Effect

In my view, cause and effect permeate every action, decision, and outcome we come across. Simply called the cause and effect theory, the "cause" refers to the reason behind anything happening, while the "effect" is the consequence of something that happened. When we peruse it, we begin to notice how this theory is intricately woven around us.

For instance, consider the introduction of the Bible to Africa—a powerful moment of cause and effect. The Bible, brought by colonizers, didn't simply arrive as a text; it carried along ideologies, beliefs, and moral structures that affected entire societies, leaving an indelible mark on culture and spirituality.

As we read the Bible, Genesis offers a fundamental narrative on the origins of humanity with Adam and Eve. According to the story, Adam was created first, followed by Eve, who was meant to help him tend to the Garden of Eden.

While God went on to create animals and bring order to the world, Adam and Eve were left to tend to the garden. However, we are not sure about their perception of knowledge. Do they possess the knowledge or wisdom to fully grasp the implications of God's command?

Before leaving them in the garden, God issued a single directive: they could freely eat from every tree except one—the tree of the knowledge of good and evil. Herein lies a pivotal cause: the creation of Adam and Eve with a specific prohibition. Had they not been there, had that tree not existed, there would be no question of obedience, no dilemma of choice. In their very existence lies the cause, and in their decision lies the effect, a sequence as timeless and universal as cause and effect itself.

Another fundamental cause in the story of Adam and Eve was that God left them in the garden. If Adam and Eve truly lacked knowledge or discernment, one might question why God didn't stay with them to guide them directly, ensuring they followed the instructions and consumed only the proper fruit from the permissible tree.

This absence of God let the chaos take place, letting the world come into being: left to navigate the garden on their own, Adam and Eve ultimately ate from the forbidden tree, choosing a path that brought knowledge and consequence. The impact of this decision ripples outward, marking a point that the creation of the two was the cause.

The story of Adam and Eve serves as an early blueprint for cause and effect, a narrative that mirrors how choices reverberate through generations. From this initial transgression, we enter a "fallen" world—a place shaped by that first act, where the consequences of their choice echo, affecting every facet of life to this day.

Looking at more recent history, particularly within African American communities, we can see how similar patterns emerge. Drugs seeping into these neighborhoods stand as a modern example of cause and effect. The arrival of drugs, whether through external forces or other systemic means, became a cause, leading to widespread addiction, fractured families, and higher rates of confinement. People often found themselves entangled in a cycle that seemed beyond their control, underscoring how cause and effect can unfold, especially when you lose control over anything.

In situations where we lack control, cause and effect becomes a chain reaction, each step inevitably leading to the next. The circumstances of life, whether as ancient as the Garden of Eden or as contemporary as the challenges faced in underserved communities, reveal how cause and effect are constants, shaping paths and altering lives.

In many communities, particularly lower-income and marginalized ones, the arrival of drugs was beyond residents' control, yet it forced them to adapt in ways they had never anticipated. Families found themselves working around the presence of drugs, focusing on keeping food on the table, roofs over their heads, and clothes on their backs. This struggle uncovers a harsh reality: for many, life becomes a constant negotiation with the consequences of external forces beyond their influence. Cause and effect lie at the heart of this cycle, an inescapable sequence where each cause precedes an inevitable effect, shaping daily life and future generations alike.

A similar pattern emerges with the liquor stores around every corner in these communities. The density of such stores on nearly every corner, within close proximity to lower-income neighborhoods, adds another layer of challenge.

For someone trying to stop drinking, help another quit, or simply encourage a loved one to avoid alcohol, the environment itself becomes an obstacle. With access so readily available, resisting temptation can feel like an uphill battle, reinforcing how cause and effect operate even in matters of personal choice.

When we recognize the weight of cause and effect in our lives, we are compelled to question whether life is, in fact, predetermined. If events are driven by causes that yield inevitable effects, is there room for true free will? To be preordained would mean knowing what is to come, understanding that the "cause" already exists, and so does its outcome (the effect). If this logic holds, one might argue that free will becomes an illusion, as the course of our lives could be guided by forces outside our control. This perspective invites us to look more closely at the very nature of choice, examining whether life is indeed a series of autonomous actions or merely a chain of inevitable reactions.

Why did Jesus know to set a dinner table using bread and fish, but god didn't?

Affordable Housing

The current housing system in the United States does more than provide shelter—it often curbs the opportunity that may appear and creates an endless loop of poverty, creating an uphill battle for those who rely on it. For many low-income families, accessing housing assistance is often concocted with many conditions and criteria that sometimes they feel like more of an obstacle rather than support. These structural issues reveal how deeply the system is flawed, leaving people in a hamster's wheel of survival.

One of the first challenges begins with the application process itself. Families applying for low-income housing have to fall under a certain criterion. For instance, any adult in the household must often have a clean criminal record, which immediately excludes many individuals from stable housing. Those who do manage to qualify are usually required to have little or no income as a way to prioritize needs. But this creates a paradox: to qualify, you must have minimal resources, yet to maintain your home, you need sufficient income. This contradiction makes families constantly balance on a tightrope between eligibility and financial survival.

Once families are accepted, they are assigned units that often have minimal amenities and are located in neglected neighborhoods. In essence, the housing assistance system becomes less about providing stable shelter and more about trapping families in environments where they have few paths forward.

The Trap of Employment and Income

When adults in these households consider working to improve their financial situation, they're often forced to make impossible choices. For families on housing vouchers, any increase in income is met with an increase in rent, creating a significant financial burden. For every extra dollar they earn, they have to pay an increased monthly rent, reducing their incentive to work more or earn higher wages. As a result, many voucher recipients are compelled to work part-time or limit their earnings to avoid crossing the income threshold that would strip them of their housing assistance.

As an example, I came across an African family that was surviving in this notorious housing system. The only adult in the family decided to work some extra hours to support their family's financial condition. They reported their current income, which resulted in the reassessment of their rent. Unfortunately, their revised income was slightly, if not significantly, above the threshold, and they had to bear the hike in their rent. If they didn't comply, they feared that they might be completely stripped off the support. This forces families into a constant game of balancing hours, wages, and expenses, trapping them in a cycle where earning too much risks losing the very support they rely on. This punitive approach to income discourages families from striving for better financial circumstances, as they are penalized for trying to improve their situation.

If they do lose the voucher, the consequences are severe. Families are often left scrambling for new housing with limited savings, little access to credit, and, frequently, no safety net. Without stable employment, they can't qualify for a conventional lease, but with a job, they may exceed the income restrictions for low-income housing. This catch-22 pushes families dangerously close to homelessness, where the only options are to start the application process over again or face life without adequate shelter.

The System's Impact on Families and Children

The instability of housing assistance affects families brutally. Constantly shifting income requirements and unpredictable rent increases disrupt the lives of children who rely on stability for academic success, social development, and emotional well-being. Children in these families are mostly left with the option of attending schools in underfunded districts. This lack of educational access only deepens the generational impact of housing insecurity as children struggle to break free from the limitations imposed on their families.

Beyond education, the lingering stress of constantly living with financial uncertainty and housing insecurity can erode family unity. The system puts the families in places where community support is scarce, depriving them of growth and resilience. When families have to move frequently, children are uprooted from familiar environments, severing ties with friends, mentors, and community organizations. This ingrains instability that can last a lifetime, making it harder for individuals to form the supportive social networks that are essential to overcoming adversity.

Perpetuating Poverty Through Policy

The fundamental flaw of the affordable housing system lies in its design—a structure that seems more focused on controlling poverty than eradicating it. The system's policies, which restrict income growth and force families to choose between economic stability and shelter, create a kind of invisible confinement. This is not a supportive network; it is a system that enforces dependency and limits upward mobility, contradicting the very concept of assistance.

To truly support families in need, housing policies must evolve to encourage financial independence and stability rather than penalize progress. This means reimagining the way assistance is calculated so that increases in income allow for gradual rent adjustments without risking eviction or voucher loss. By implementing policies that promote upward mobility, families would have the opportunity to achieve self-sufficiency, reducing the cycle of dependency and paving the way for future generations to thrive.

The Mask of Policy

"They call it policy," they say, but what it really means is "Do as we say or face the consequences." That's the system in its truest form—disguising control as courtesy, shoving you into a corner, and calling it procedure. No matter how polite or respectful you try to be, they'll push your buttons, test your patience, and then pretend their hands are clean.

But here's the truth: the system only has power until we let them have it. For too long, rules and regulations have been built against you, meeh, and anyone who dares to think differently. That's why we must stand—stand tall, speak loud, and speak the truth. Change doesn't happen quietly; it starts with a voice. Your voice. You might think the world won't notice, but the moment you see yourself as the world—as the big thing—it all shifts. They'll hear you then, *AY FREE~MEEH!*

Contraps and Freewill

The Illusion of Freedom

I never paid much attention to the idea of free will. It always sounded too abstract, too distant—like one of those words that people just say but don't evidently perpetuate. Free will, to me, is supposed to mean doing what you want without fear of punishment. But does anyone really have that? That kind of free will? They said we were born with it, the autonomy over our life, that it's a gift. But I disagree. How can it be free when every choice comes with judgment, and judgment is almost always followed by punishment?

This punishment doesn't even necessarily need to come from some mysterious higher power in the sky. No, it happens right here, on this very bordered land we walk on every day. It comes in whispers from our neighbors, in disapproving glances, in the way society quietly reshapes our lives without asking. We're told we have free will, but we're pushed, pulled, and punished at every turn.

A World of Papers—Contraps

Then there are the contracts. Pieces of paper tainted with black ink with a mark at the bottom where a just a little scribble will strip us of our autonomy and our rights, binding us to terms and rules we didn't create. Every time I'm asked to sign one, it feels like my free will is slipping right through my fingers like sand on the beach escaping from our gripping toes. What's the point of signing all these papers after all? To me, they're nothing but tools of control, holding us hostage in a system that's already severed.

Think about it. Walk into any business, any office, and what's the first thing they hand you? Paper. From the leasing office, where you sign your life away for a roof over your head, to the grocery store, where a receipt is pressed into your hand, we are drowning in paper. And for what? Half of it turns out to be useless junk the moment we step away. It's as if these pieces of paper have become the currency of our captivity.

The Trap of Applications

And don't get me started on applications. Those forms are the worst kind of trickery. They ask questions they already know the answers to, pretending to care about what we think. But it's not about us, is it? It's about trapping us in their system, making sure we play by their rules. The questions are just bait, and the moment you submit, they've got you. It's like the system is always one step ahead, watching, waiting, ready to pounce the moment you try to break free.

These papers, these contracts—they're not about choice. They're about control. They don't liberate us; they ensnare us. That's why I don't call them contracts. I call them *contraps*. Because that's what they are: traps dressed up in fancy language, a camouflage, with just enough space for you to scribble your name at the bottom.

What If We Refused?

Sometimes, I wonder what would happen if we all just stopped signing. What if we said, "No more," and refused to play their games? Would they still call it free will, or would they show their true colors? The penalties would pile up, that's for sure. They'd do everything in their power to remind us that refusing is not an option and is out of the question. That's the irony of it all. They tell us we're free, but the moment we exercise that so-called freedom, we're punished for it.

What kind of freedom is that? It's not freedom at all. It's a façade, a cruel joke played on people who just want to live their lives without fear of judgment or consequences.

The People Just Want to Be Free

I know this much: the people just want to be free. Truly free. Not the kind of freedom that comes with little mysterious strings attached, but the kind that lets you breathe without feeling the weight of someone else's expectations. The kind that lets you walk through life without signing your name away to something you don't believe in.

But how do we search for that kind of freedom in a world built on contraps? Maybe the first step is to stop believing in the papers, to stop giving them power over our lives. Maybe it's time to reclaim what's been taken from us. Because if free will is real, then it's ours to take back. And if it's not, then it's time to create something new— something better.

Misunderstood

Waking Up to the Truth

Every day, it feels like we're calling out to each other, jolting one another from a deep slumber. "Wake up," we say, sometimes with urgency, sometimes with love. But is waking up as simple as fluttering your eyes open or actually stepping out of the state of oblivion? It's terrifying to realize that the life you've been living, the truths you've held onto, might all have been a big illusion. That's a hard pill to swallow.

Yet, when you truly wake up, it's not all fear—it's also freedom. The clarity hits you like fresh air, filling your lungs and reminding you of your power. It's amazing to feel that shift, to see the world with new eyes. But the journey doesn't end there. Because the moment you start to see clearly, the world starts to see *you* differently. And not always in a good way.

The Loneliness of Being Misunderstood

Freedom always comes with a price; being misunderstood is part of the process. It's inevitable. You can try to explain and try to share what you've learned, but some people won't want to hear it. It's not because they're incapable of understanding; it's because your truth frightens them. It is one of the most terrifying things for a person living in shadows and strapped in chains to unlearn what they were taught. Accepting what you've discovered means they would have to reevaluate everything they've believed in. That's like shedding the old skin to make room for the new one. It's easier for them to dismiss you than to face the possibility that they, too, have been living in an illusion.

But here's the thing: not everyone will misunderstand you. The *right* people will see you, hear you, and understand. They may be few and far between, but they're out there. They will find you and seek you.

The Process of Unlearning

The journey of waking up and understanding is like learning to walk all over again. It's messy, it's raw, and it's humbling. Imagine being a baby, taking those first unsteady steps. When you've believed something false for so long, and the truth finally reveals itself, it can feel like your world is crumbling. Everything you thought was solid turns to dust, leaving you raw and exposed, bawling like a baby who's lost their footing.

But that's part of it, too—the breaking down before the building up. The pain before the power. Waking up is not just about seeing the illusion; it's about learning to move past it, to rebuild your understanding of the world on a foundation that's real.

From Practice to Power

From *meeh* to you: keep practicing. Keep holding on to what you know in the pit of your soul to be true. There will be moments when it feels like the world is against you, but those moments are just stepping stones. Keep moving forward, and you'll realize that the power to shape your reality was within you all along.

Before you know it, you'll look around and see that the world is no longer something that happens *to* you—it's something that happens *with* you. It is here to grow with you, inhabitate you. You're not just living in it; you're shaping it, holding it in your hands, with all its peculiarity and beauty.

Embrace the Process

Being misunderstood is not the end—it's the beginning. The beginning of understanding yourself, finding your people, and living your truth. It's scary, yes. But it's also exhilarating. So, keep waking up. Keep growing. And trust that the process, however difficult, will lead you exactly where you're meant to be.

The System and Meeh

Speak Your Mind, Change Your World

I cannot stress it enough: speak your mind. Fear has kept us silent for too long, but fear isn't what we're here for. We are saviors in our own right, here to challenge what's wrong and make room for what's right. Change doesn't come from saying "yes" to everything; it comes from being brave enough to say "no" when it matters.

The truth is, the system has trained us to fear change, to believe it's dangerous or impossible. But change is where greatness lies. Every step forward, every new possibility, is built on the courage of those who came before us. They walked hard roads so we could march forward. No, we don't move backward. We move ahead. And every time we do, we honor those voices—those warriors—who refused to be silenced.

Forward Together

The system wants us to feel small, to feel like we don't matter, but that's the illusion. It's time we remember who we are and what we stand for. Speak up not just for yourself but for everyone who can't. Each voice is a ripple, and together, we're the wave.

So, don't hold back. Speak. Stand. Believe. Because the system only wins if we forget we're the big thing. And trust, we are bigger than anything they can imagine.

Poems For You

The Afreecan Woman

Rooted in Africa

The Afreecan woman carries the essence of her homeland wherever she goes. She may find herself in the West, surrounded by a different culture and rhythm, but her roots remain deeply planted in the sacred soil of Africa. She is more than her beauty; she is sacred, spiritual, and strong—a living connection to the lineage of her ancestors.

When a man encounters a woman like her, he sees beyond her slanted dark brown eyes or her soft, chocolate skin. Her curly brown hair holds the stories of generations, and her very presence carries the warmth of the sun and the resilience of the earth. To love her is not just to love a woman but to embrace the strength, wisdom, and spirit of an entire history.

Loving a Diamond

To love an Afreecan woman is a privilege, but it is also a responsibility. She is like a diamond, precious and rare, discovered and cherished for her purity and brilliance. But this treasure comes with an expectation: to be honest, loyal, and trustworthy. A man who dares to love her must meet her with his whole heart, for she gives nothing less of herself.

When a man just laid his eyes on a Goddess. Her attention; it is not just the beginning of a relationship; it is the start of a legacy. Together, they embark on a journey—a partnership that blossoms into a family, children growing under the guidance of their love. But love, like diamonds, is not without its pressures.

The Afreecan woman's trust is sacred but also extremely fragile. When the man reveals his hidden flaw it shakes the foundation of her being. This revelation doesn't just hurt; it shatters her. Her trust, once resolute, begins to waver, and uncertainty takes root.

He dismisses her pain, believing it's just her emotions running wild. But what he doesn't realize is that he has awakened a storm within her. The betrayal cuts deeply, wounding her heart, soul, and body in ways he cannot comprehend. Her pain becomes a force, rippling outward, not just affecting the two of them but touching the fabric of humanity itself.

Her vulnerability is not a weakness—it is a reaction as natural and powerful as the earth responding to imbalance. Like nature in turmoil, her spirit rises, her strength surges, and she becomes a force he cannot contain. In her pain, she mirrors the world's own moment of stillness, like the silence that overtook 2020, putting the world to a halt. If it could, it would have stopped the rotation of the Earth, too, closing her heart and soul in the same way the world seemed to shut down.

But in this closing, there is also a realization. She is more than special; she is irreplaceable. The man finally sees what he has lost—a woman whose value cannot be gauged, a woman whose ancestors walk with her, guarding her spirit.

A Lesson in Loss

The Afreecan woman, once open and loving, has now withdrawn, leaving the man to understand the magnitude of his mistake. He will not meet another like her, for she is not just one woman—she is the embodiment of generations, the reflection of her ancestors' strength and resilience.

To lose her is not just to lose a partner; it is to lose a connection to something much greater. And as she moves forward, carrying her pain but also her power, the man is left behind, learning that a diamond, once fractured, will never be the same again.

The Afreecan Man

A Man Like No Other

Dang! How did we end up here, with the Afreecan man? I can't help but wonder what it took to deserve someone so extraordinary. A man who moves through life with purpose, a man who can guide you with wisdom, protect you without question, and love you without limits. This is not just any man—this is a man who carries the weight of history and the light of the future.

When he walks into a room, the energy shifts. He doesn't have to say a word; you can feel his presence. He is the kind of man who knows he is the light, and because of that, it's always his time to shine. It's not arrogance—it's assurance. It's knowing that his place in the world is earned, not given.

The Quiet Storm

He is low-key, but don't let that fool you. Beneath the quiet exterior lies a spirit that is loud and ferocious when it needs to be. He doesn't waste energy on foolishness, and he won't let it near you either. He sees the value in a woman, the strength, the beauty, the potential. And because of that, he'll protect you from the fools who are ignorant to the fragility that comes with women.

A Man of Forgiveness and Strength

The *Afreecan* man as I like to call him, doesn't just love; he understands. He knows that women, like men, are imperfect, and yet he loves with a patience so rare. He forgives gently, not out of weakness, but out of strength. And when the time is right, he'll let you know—because he's not just leading; he's teaching.

This man doesn't just want a partner or a caretaker to walk behind his shadows; he wants a teammate. He keeps you in his game, not as a spectator but as a player, because he sees your potential. He builds with you, not above you, creating something that lasts—a bond that feels ancient, like it's been here since the beginning of this world, yet remains new and alive.

A King, A Best Friend, A Rare Gem

He is more than a partner; he is a king. A true king. A man who stands tall in his convictions and soft in his love. He's not just someone to walk beside; he's someone to trust, someone to lean on, someone to grow with. He is your best friend when life gets tough and your greatest cheerleader when you rise.

He's a rare gem, shining with a brilliance that doesn't fade. A man whose presence feels like the world finally makes sense, like everything is right where it should be. That's the Afreecan man—a light in the dark, a guide through life, and a love that transforms everything it touches.

Brave one

You're smarter than you think.

I can look at you and I wink.

Plant your feet in the ground.

When you stand make a sound

Let them see your strength.

When you teach, teach from within

There are generations waiting on you.

Find out where it starts, is it with the WHO?

A FREE~MEEH.